TELL ME ABOUT GOD

Library of Congress Catalog Card Number 90-72103
© 1991, The STANDARD PUBLISHING Company, Cincinnati, Ohio
Division of STANDEX INTERNATIONAL Corporation. Printed in U.S.A.

TELL ME ABOUT GOD

written by Linda Talbert Humble

illustrated by Suzanne Cruise

"Mommy, Mommy,
Can you tell me, please,

Who put the leaves
On the big, tall trees?

"The leaves make nice shade
When the cool breezes blow.
And I can watch bugs
Crawling fast or slow.

"Who makes the little bugs
To have crawling legs and feet?

Do you think they would tell me,
If only they could speak?

"Who wakes the sun each morning
And tells it to start a new day?

Its brightness makes me happy.
That's why I run and play.

"Who makes it rain
So flowers will grow,

And I can splash in puddles
And the rivers can flow?

"And who paints the rainbow
After it rains,

Then saves all the colors
And uses them again?

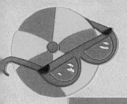

"Who tells the geese
Which way to fly

To find the warm sun
When winter fills the sky?

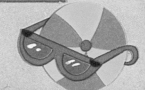

"Who gives the birds
Their songs to sing,

So I can hear music
When I sit in my swing?

"Who puts the warm sand
At the edge of the sea,
So I can build castles
As high as can be?

"Who tells the cows
What they must do,

So I can have milk
And ice cream too?

"Who lets the moon
Give just enough light,

So I won't be afraid
In my bed at night?

"Mommy, Mommy,
Can you tell me, please?
I want to know the answers
To questions like these."

"God is the answer,
And this helps us to see
That He does all these things
Because He loves you and me."